OCHO #22

Edited by Miguel Murphy

A Publication of

MiPOesias Magazine
www.mipoesias.com
Bloomington, Illinois

Cover art by I.M. Bess
OCHO Series editor Didi Menendez

CONTENTS

OCHO #22

Introduction

DEAR AMERICA, DON'T BE MY VALENTINE

The call for this edition of OCHO went out as a response to several political events in the Fall-Winter season of 2008-2009. The first, a moment in the Vice Presidential debates early November between Governor Sarah Palin and Senator Joe Biden, in which both candidates seemed to befriend the gay community while denouncing our right to marry. What an awful laughter relieved both the candidates and the audience, as if everyone were too embarrassed to discuss the validity of a gay relationship in the national discussion. Then, the passing of propositions 8 in California, 102 in Arizona, and Amendment 2 in Florida changing state constitutions and making it illegal for gays to marry. This historic election brought with it the disappointment and dissolution of 18,000 marriages and families directly affected by the Prop. 8 vote in California and, in Arkansas, an amendment making it illegal for gay couples to adopt. We in the gay community found ourselves heartbroken the same night President Obama was elected, and at his recent inauguration, the invitation of homophobic evangelical minister Rick Warren incited further unrest. It seemed hypocritical to many of us that Warren be invited to give a national prayer after publicly speaking against the gay lifestyle, equating it with pedophilia, denouncing our relationships as immoral, sinful and criminal.

My call went out, using the vulgar expletive and offensive language of stereotypes for queer persons as a way to demonstrate, as I stated in a guest blog for the Poetry Foundation website, that separate is not equal. If we cannot use the same language to describe and to name our long term relationships—and because the use of the word *partner* denies that our relationships are spiritual pursuits—then we are relegated to the language that has been accepted by culture at large, language that has presumed to know, and to abuse, the sanctity of these relationships:

> *Dear Fags, Dikes, Trannies, Transvestites, He-she's, She-*
> *males, Tomboys and Mamas-boys, Lesbos, Fudge-packers,*
> *Muff-divers, Bears, Twinks and Closet Freaks, Butch and*
> *Lipstick, Hairdresser or Harley-rider, Republican, Democrat,*
> *Independent, Green—Dear family, dear people of color and*

9

other,

This is a call for queer poetry, essays on poetics, and reviews of works by queer poets for the February 2009 OCHO edition: DEAR AMERICA, DON'T BE MY VALENTINE.

Your work does not have to address the politics of this post. The purpose of this issue is to highlight and bring together a strong sampling of diverse work by queer authors in the contemporary American poetry scene.

Some people misunderstood my use of the derogative, and I received a surprising number of emails from gay poets saying as much. I was called silly, ranting, angry, and told that I was sending the wrong message, though exactly to whom no one ever specified. My point was that without access to the word "marriage", what we are left with is this language of inequality. I felt we must assume our identity under the banner of these insults in order to pronounce our equality—we must be acknowledged as we are—illicitly—and still be able to assume the rights of the word "marriage".

This is not to say I wanted to edit a compilation of a particular kind of poem. In fact, I was more curious than anything to know who unknown gay poets were, poets like myself early in their writing lives—I wanted to know what gay men and gay women were writing, and what their writing looked like. What is the struggle of their poem, I wondered, in its obsession and its craft?

I made no solicitations, though some poets I know are printed here. And though it could have been relatively easy to ask well-established or prominent mid- to late- career gay poets, both men and women, to contribute, I felt it important to rely on the relatively unknown community. I wanted to know poets I didn't already know. I wanted those of us unspoken for. So I relied on word of mouth, the blogposted invitation, and hoped for the best. Here, then, are 17 gay men and 12 gay women whose work for me best represents what I received during the last 3 months.

I accepted everything I could in good conscience. I was not trying to propose what a "gay" poetry should look like. In fact, there are readers who will look here and find poems not to their liking, poems too sentimental, vulgar, abstract, melodramatic, or worse, too self-indulgent, and who will turn their noses up. I can say that as an editor I looked to each submission with a curious ear. I wanted to be as inclusive of style and approach and risk as possible. These are poems of politics and desire, loss and memory, history and fable, faith and contemplation, and, almost invariably, they are about love.

It felt as if gay men and women were compelled to address love more than anything, as if the love poem were a preoccupation we had to pursue, were compelled to make our own. One responsibility of the love poem is that it weigh pleasure against politics, that eros is given freedom to fulfill itself. I was most interested in these poems how each poet worked to fulfill a voice of eros against the trappings of a social and homophobic realm. The result, of course, is the freedom of the poem.

This issue began in a moment of frustration and political activism—a moment in which I demanded to know who would stand together with me and be seen, who would stand with me under the banner of our given insults and demand a parity for the language of "marriage", and thereby demand an institutionalized recognition of our equality. It has resulted in a process that, for me, has been a drawing together of a diverse community of poets who I am grateful now to stand with, as I am grateful to witness this desired collection of poems at their struggle.

Miguel Murphy
Venice Beach, California
February 2009

Brian Leary

Defense of the Realm

> A thousand pigeons, each with a two-ounce explosive capsule, landed at
> intervals on a specific target might be a seriously inconvenient surprise.
> – *Lea Rayner, Head of the Pigeon Policy Committee, UK, WWII*

So welcome to the kingdom

of the wrong way to love. The king is locked high
in a tower, singing—that fey, red-cere bird—& the rest of us, we're

donning hedonism like armor, braving
the little explosions beneath each new man's fingertips. I mean, what

would you do? Which do you think
is the more condemnable shame—looking or not

looking? Me? Here I am
forgetting *who am I fighting against—why care who's*
the more masculine man?

So here I am unable home.
Here I am failing

the art of not falling for you: can't help it—

a flight of pigeons keeps flapping up from my skin: can't help it—
it's heave-ho!, duck-duck-goose, discombobulate

downtrod upswing & hubbub: can't help it—chorus of
hey bird-lover, hey rock dove,
buck up, boy, 'cause some real good shit's about to go off.

Elizabeth J. Colen

Diving Lessons

You longed for that perfect affliction, the one you didn't see in yourself. Blind and rattling through the undergrowth, a ground vole comes up for air. You choke too to see the earth against his face, soot-covered nose, eyes sewn over. You thought once of being an astronaut, a pilot, deep-sea diver, or if nothing else a shipwrecked mess left. You thought some distance from the ground zero of it all would do you good. But once you left dirt, the muscle of your lungs stopped. In the hum of twin engines, the thin air made you bleed, blood-shot, your head thrown back. In the quiet of the ocean, like the violence of the dance floor, you feared the dark of every passing body. Fin slash or shirts opened like a knife cut from throat to navel. The turned up image of yourself in the bottom of the glass. *Remember to breathe.*

Matches Between Teeth

You were all summer and I was the hands in your hair. We fished off
the yellow pier or, I should say, you fished off the pier while I
watched from the trees. You were never me enough but I made do
with you. I made us lie side by side mimicking each other's limbs
until we were fooled by mirror or fire. I conspired to get you to live
with me. I got rid of your mail, I lost your dog, your mother, your
shoes, I trained them to love again and then set them all free. You
were washing dishes with your back to me, saying something about
fireflies or mosquitoes. You told me to shut the screen. I turned your
neighbors out of their homes, checked all the attics for sparrows,
then set the first blaze.

Earthly Delights

> *The world is merely a failed study.*
> —Vincent van Gogh

It's not all vomiting.
There's music & bread

baking.
The metronome, the harp, the butcher
knife & all those other dangers
not always so obvious.

But there's Kenneth
Cole & MAC lip-liner.
It's not just
funerals & life

support systems whirring
& beeping. Nor is it fucking

among the songbirds, gigantic
as Macy's parade balloons, & berries
the size of Volkswagens. There's Queen
Anne's Lace in the meadows,

as though some mad auntie's
scattered her drawers of doilies.
The noises & cries of the damned

& dying doppler here; the please
please please my grandmother whimpered,
& I knew she wanted water;

she was starving & I gave it. & later I tried
to make that moment lovely: & I failed.
But there's thirty-three flavors
of hot and cold running porn,

Rihanna, basset hounds, & scotch.
Listen: I'm just a man
who loves the pieces of the world:
the isolate, jagged, & ugly.
There's more if you want,

of everything; & even more
of what you cannot stand; but you can leave
what you like: a slice of lemon
chiffon cake; another man's palm
on your cheek in the night;

along the one lane road,
a stand of wild bergamot.

With You As Vincent

Call it profusion, explosion, seduction: these flowers
        erect: the black prince, the rebel boy, the maximillian
        sunflowers, the wild horses, the stargazers.
Their waves and scent dependent on the wind. Even the nettle-

leaved mullein, its fleshy petals the color of the flesh of your groin.
        How much the earth accommodates, it can accept.
        Forget the stalks, the foliage: forget the show:
go to the root. How busy the dirt: its beetles, its grubs,

its very upheavals. It holds tight, like you; takes my fingers
        as readily. Is that too far? To say you are the earth?
        Perhaps. Better to say: you look like a self portrait:
with your burr cut and beard, that splash of ejaculate

in your mustache shining
like the last gasp of a starry night.

Whittle

To defy the structure of his body;

to starve it down until purely frame;

to prime it for bursting;

to go go go—
he took white crosses,
dexedrine, until he trembled
in the mirror. He found himself
beautiful, ruthless and shark-like.

He thought it
predatory, clever;

he thought of that Shakespeare line,
the one from Caesar: 'that lean
& hungry look;' he

found a sort of jesus
in the gnaw of his belly;
a cleanliness in wanting

denied. To be the last of summer:

like milkweed, tomatoes

ripening until collapse

of flesh then issuance of seed

unto the air and earth.

He loved the lines, the relief,
the rise of his own bones.

Carol Guess

Was It Love,

that secret war? Or plastic? Were we undressing for an audience of gold stars? Were we blizzards of skin flaking off into identical snowflakes? Were we patterned after Greek myths or God? Were we barrettes in slippery blonde? Were we a globe spun round too quickly? Were we consequence-slash-catastrophe? Were we witches, spells cast as bombs? Were we fear? Were we mirrors and smoke? Were we democracy or a meaningless joke? Were we a witness in that pet shop in Baghdad? Were we the man, the bird, the cage? Were we Mohannad al-Azawi, Sunni? His body, legs hogtied, drilled full of holes.

Dahlia

You wanted *up up up* and then it found us. Landline, treeline, skyline—wings cutting green and the spaces between us. Not silence but a throaty hum. Lessons stopped and started on a prayer, but I wondered who was listening. Could we be sure of the dirt god Duwamish, holding our plane aloft on his raft? Stopped on the bridge, you dropped my key into Lake Union. Gas Works Park shed rust over dry docks, hills rolling dirt down schoolkids' socks. There's a name for this feeling and it sounds like your name. Amity—I want to hear you say it. I've sent you letters but they come back stumped, stamped defunct. I hope you're writing to me. There's a cruel pink scar on my shoulder, dahlia. People fall. We fell, that's all. *God of Missing Pieces have mercy on me* in the City of Minor Ghosts in a minor key.

White Rock

Flyaway first, birds lifting the tree. Breakfast, plates shift, and the cafe shudders. We cling to the counter, counting afters. This isn't the city we were born to. We're just two girls who traverse borders. The clerk rolls each finger through ink onto paper—crossing out *groom*, writing *bride #2*. Nobody notices us, but we do. This isn't a lullaby but facts stacked like dishes. One thousand white crosses stain Peace Arch Park. Border guards search our car for cherries. Our license dissolves as we trundle through Blaine. Optimism of planes overhead—low thrum of war scatters deer down Mount Baker. The whole town's hiding, dodging discourse with cellphone ringtones. It's just us in our trousseaus on Railroad. The avenue stretches as far as its drugs. Red lights, bail bonds, dark drop, crunk. *We Will Not Be Undersold.* International rumspringa away from the cube. From the start we promise no tattoos.

Jeremy Halinen

Dear Laramie, Dear Liar, Dear Once Upon a Time

Matt and I were walking hand
in hand down University Avenue,
sipping sweet tea in bright light
sent about eight minutes before
by the sun, sweet nothings
slipping
now and again
from our lips,
which couldn't have been more
calm,
when two frat boys
approached us with lazy
grins on the faces
below the brims of their hats.

We nodded at them
as we passed.

That night, we drove out of town,
parked at the edge of a field
and made love awhile
by a split-rail fence
in light sent long before we were born
by some stars.

Buggering You under an Apple Tree

how like an inflated
earth
you are
apple
of my why
and i
globe of airplanes cars
and throwing
stars passing in and in
your handsome
gate
am hardly planet yet enough
to bear your skinsoft weight

Christine Leclerc

Wolf

1

Wolf walked past a small haystack at dawn.
He'd been up all night huffing in the woods beyond the meadow.
Tree sap, bird's nests, rusted car parts, assorted eyeballs:
these things he huffed.

There was a pig in a house made of sticks nearby.
Her house was a densely woven globe of branches.
There was a branch from every tree in the woods.
And it made Wolf huff to find the smell of woods in a meadow.

He ran to her house to huff bark off the branches
and woke the pig with his kerfuffle. She leapt out of
her bed of shed feathers and put her eye to the peephole—
yanked it away at the sight of Wolf huffing.

The wolf stood back and watched as the nest rocked
free from its foundation. He watched the nest roll down
to the river. And when he looked at where the house had been
he saw some foil, which he huffed and nearly choked on.

Wolf howled in panic and the foil fell to the ground.
He sat down to catch his breath and saw a hole where the foil had been.
It was the size for wolves to crawl in. So Wolf entered
because he was sick of being aboveground with so much to huff on.

Wolf weighs the pros and cons of huffing, quietly, to himself.

WOLF
What I like about huffing:

- Hearing myself make shit-loads of noise
- Making so much noise that no one else exists
- How it feels when I huff the right thing

What I don't like about huffing:
- Not knowing what to huff
- Feeling desperate and out of control
- Feeling alone

The hole was a tunnel and Wolf crept along on his stomach
until noon. His stomach kept getting warmer and he wondered
if he was close to the earth's molten core.
Then from above there was light.

And the wolf saw a grate that held up a fire.
And he got as close as he could and smelled pig and corn muffin
through the wood smoke. And Wolf had to huff
and the fire blazed. Embers fell and seared Wolf's insides.

At this Pig ran to the hearth. He could see Wolf's snout
through the flames with his one unhuffed eye. He threw a log on.
And Wolf wailed, "Let me out, YOU FUCKING FAGGOT!"

So the pig ate his muffin on the patio.

Wolf crackled. He backed out of the tunnel.
"I'll find that pig when I get out and huff his ears off," Wolf sniveled.
He went back and back and back until he was out. Only,
he was nowhere near the where the branch house had been.

When he looked up he saw a castle. He went up the hillside and saw
that the moat was filled in and the drawbridge was missing.
The words *HUGEST LOSERS* were written above the entrance
and *YOU CAN'T NOT BEGET US* was cobbled into the walkway.

Wolf saw *I ♥ Freddy Mercury* in gold letters on a stone by the entrance
and thought the other words must be fag humor. There was a can of
gold paint by his feet. He went to throw it at the wall, but then he realized
his vandalism would only add to the castle's beauty.

Just kidding.

2

Wolf didn't realize anything. The real reason for his not
throwing the can is that two little pigs in wedding gowns arrived on the scene.
They leapt out of a horse-drawn carriage shouting, "That's paint! Not throw!"
And: "There's a paintbrush next to the rifle."

Then the tall one ran back into the carriage and came out with a football.
"Here's something to throw," she said, launching it into the air.
The ball went far and Wolf chased it. He hadn't played football
since high school. But it was all coming back to him now.

The ball was going, going. It kept on going, until it stopped
and dropped into Wolf's arms. He sat down to catch his breath
and looked at the castle whose walls seemed to be rearranging
themselves. And the writing changed, but he was too far to read it.

Wolf could see the wives playing frisbee on the front lawn with their
pet corgis. He wanted to huff the frisbee, but it was too far, so he
huffed the football. He wanted to huff a corgi. Then it rained
and the tall pig ran to and from the carriage, unloading groceries.

When the rain stopped there was a rainbow. Muffins sprung
from the ground and covered the hill. Wolf could see that the horse
was chomping on some corn muffins and watching Wolf with one eye.

And Wolf thought he ought to go live with his brother for a while.

Julie R. Enszer

SEEING ANNIE LIEBOVITZ'S *A PHOTOGRAPHER'S LIFE 1990-2006*

When I walk in already I am angry
about Susan "the long-term friend."
Another for whom the study of gay men,
fashionable, but pussy-licking lesbians
are to be denied. Even the obituary
reads only, *she is survived by a son
and a sister.* Three years later,
Annie concedes, "Yes, you could say we were
lesbians, though it is not a word Susan
would use—" and here she pauses, "or approve."
So when I see Susan in the small photos,
snapshots amid outsized glitz and poised glamour
enlarged to be bigger than any one life,
she peers out at me as if from a small
cabinet or cupboard, cramped,
not even large enough to be a closet,
while Annie pins these pictures in a barn,
listening to Rosanne Cash, crying. She lives on.
So I soften to Susan. Her cancer-wizened face,
shaved head, tired eyes. I want her bookshelves,
filled and ordered. I want her trip to France and Jordan,
but most of all, I want her to use my words,
which now she will never do.

Cunts

For Tee Corinne

Three hours before Tee Corinne died
I was in a grange in Vermont for a poetry reading,
I started with poems about social justice —
what the organizer wanted —
but it was heavy and, dare I say, dour
so I ended with one that had always been
a crowd favorite about sex in my fantasy single life
only I had forgotten that I always read it
to queer audiences and this audience was
definitely not queer and the poem contains
both the "p word" and the "f word"
my wife hadn't forgotten and she,
in the audience, looked on with horror
and even I, as I was reading,
realized the depth of my profanity
and read the poem more slowly thinking
could I change it? change the words?
call it my "love hatch?" insert "making love?"
but those words didn't suit the diction
so I barreled on with "eating my pussy"
and "fucking me real hard" and
when I was done I was exhausted and
the northeastern audience politely applauded and
I left flush with the power of my tongue and
my friend who was reading next
she had to slink on to the stage and
sit there in the mess of my come
and her mother and sister were there and
I felt bad about showing them all of my stuff
but in the moment, in the moment,
I felt powerful
talking about pussy

as powerful as I had felt three days earlier
when, after making love to my wife,
who was only eight hours away
from the onset of her menses and
had a deep purple lining inside her labia and vagina,
the way our bodies do when they are eager
to slough off the unnecessary lining of our womb
it was so beautiful and she was relaxed
and we were on vacation, so I said
I'd like to take a picture and she said *sure* and
I did, two actually, although they didn't capture
that deep purple in part because
she was over taken by prudery
at the last moment and
prattled on about this is how people end up
with compromising photographs on the web
or in the news and she made me swear
that I would never show them to anyone and
never, ever put them on the internet,
which is a promise I easily made
because I knew that I had the photographs,
two of them, showing her pussy, her labia
slightly separated, her clitoris swollen, erect,
I am only telling you this
because three days and three hours later
Tee Corinne died and it was because of her
that I wrote the poem and took those pictures
somehow it seems like a proper homage to her
that while she was dying
all of this was happening.
You should probably know
I have kept my promise to my wife –
no one has seen the pictures of her pussy,
but I look at them every day
and I am happy –
happy for my wife's cunt and
thankful to Tee who enabled me
to see lesbian love and cunts in color.

Scott Hightower

"Intimacy and Familiarity"

"Sleep has no spy, imagined joy no sin."
                                    Ovid

Unlike his mother who innocently
drank contaminated milk,

he went off to whittle
coffin pegs.

Later, he shared a bed
with Lamon, his body guard;

before that, in Illinois,
a bed with "low crotched" Steed;

and, after that,
with David Derickson.

In the summer
quarters of 1862,

> *... he grew to like the Bucktails,*
> *especially company K,*

with whose captain
he became so friendly

that he invited him
to share his bed

on autumn nights
when Mrs. Lincoln was away . . . ."

Wilde and Genet Bequeathed

a hemi-quadriga—

two—of whatever

they were . . . two-bit

peg boys; a slightly

more seasoned chicken

and his mate, artists who opted

to work in a house rather than

sail away and grub for blubber;

or two provincial boys

with an innate sense

of the parameters

of their ethereal voices

and the tender limits

of service or local

glamour, the charade,

the harshness of the trap

or team; two squeaky

boys by greatness

in the indelible posture

of Claire and Solange,

Blanche and Stanley,

George and Martha;

or one in the guise

of Cleopatra, Ophelia,

"Kitty Litter," Violet,

Delilah, rhapsodic Salome.

Brent Goodman

[past lives]

Redhead suicide, scarlet fever, holocaust, third rail, stillborn. Best not to blame past lives for migraines, luck, regret, or déjà vu. Haifa. Sapporo. Luxembourg. Eden. Each life learns to outlive the last. Eat rich meals, fuck, haunt museums, Eurorail every hostel from Amsterdam to Zagreb. Chalk a line around your silhouette near the fountain. Pray your children may survive you. Dear mystery: are you the outline, shadow, earth or sun?

[scars]

The glossy spooned out quarter on my calf where a tumor anointed my childhood. Or here, where a tooth sunk in. A constellation of white stars mapping the small of my back. The girl who cuts herself pulls her sleeves down. In my knee the shrapnel that pierced my father's 20's. This scar is my covenant with god. On TV the mystic blossoms red flowers from her palms, recites the rosary, opens her blouse to reveal a blood-seared cross.

C. Dale Young

Fourteen

Bless me Father, for I have sinned. It has been
six days since my last confession. I let a guy
cheat off of my science test because it made me
feel smarter. And I ignored my Mother telling me

to be home by 9:00 pm. I don't really even know
why she asks such things. And I continue to have
impure thoughts, sometimes every hour. I let a
girl kiss me, a boy, too, but we all had our clothes on.

And this may not be a sin, but I knocked Mike down
on the basketball court just as he was making a jump,
just to be able to help him up, help him back
to the locker room. His knee got twisted. It swelled

until it looked like a softball. It was so swollen.
He let me hold ice to it until his folks came.
I liked holding the ice to it. But I found myself
having impure thoughts, Father, strange thoughts.

I sat there holding the ice and staring at his knee
and up the legs of his shorts. I could see
the white edge of his jockey shorts and more.
I had to look, Father. I had to look.

Forgive me, I couldn't help it, the staring.
It was like the time last week, after the game,
when I couldn't help but watch the soap suds
under your chin just before you washed off.

I sat on a bench in my towel and watched you, the
shape of your back, your arms, your chest. I know
this is wrong, Father, watching you in the shower.
But I only watched the soap. I only watched the water.

The Fool

In the old play so many have read, the King decides
to speak to his people, one by one, directly, decides to
forego the usual intermediaries. Foolish move
on his part. The King as Fool. The fool as King.
See, the air was as crisp as it ever would be in Florida.

As close to Fall as one could find in the Sunshine State.
And it is funny how the mind can lose things, large things,
in moments of panic. Funny that, and funny the word
"overcast." But the sky was, in fact, overcast that day,
and my mind had lost my car. Running through

the Church parking lot, it was nowhere to be found.
And when I found it, I could not find my keys.
There was no one else to blame. No one else.
All of that afternoon, there was fire and brimstone
and circles of hell. And I dared not speak. I paced

my room in silence, round and round repeating
my own steps. It was as if in the repeating circles
I would find myself coming back from the other direction.
If a man lies down with another man... How those words
kept circling in my head, the priest's stern sermon.

And in my head, my own questions circled. What was I?
How could I be this "abomination"? The alligator
had no answer. The blue heron looked away.
Always looking outside. Always trying to find
an answer outside. And on the small deck, I

closed my eyes. There was no one else to blame.
And what I said, what I said out loud, surprised
even me: "God, You have got to listen to me.
No more priests. No more Holy Mother Church.
No more dark confessionals. From here on out,

it's just You and me, God. Because this abomination
is Your abomination. You can raise me up, God,
or drop me like a bad date. But I will not listen
again to a man of the cloth. Not him, not another."
And I waited for the thunder and lightning,

waited for the ground to open up and swallow
the deck, the chair, this foolish man in the chair.
But the clouds cleared. The sunlight poured over
my small deck. And the blue heron returned
to fly circle after circle around the sad fountain.

Dustin Brookshire

Meeting Judy Blume

I bought *Are you there God? It's me Margaret*,
as a giveaway for a party I was hosting.
Wondering if I should say, *Are you there Judy?*
It's me Dustin, but decided not: too cliché.
Everyone's heard of
Judy Blume,
or at least everyone who attended
a Scholastic book fair.

I waited in line patiently, feeling bad
for the other writers at the signing,
all waiting for Judy.
She had a volunteer pass us notecards.
We wrote the personalized messages
we wanted inscribed in our books.
She looked at my card—puzzlement
came across her face, as if she had passed
a puppies for sale sign
when there were kittens in the basket.
I explained, *It's a giveaway, I thought*
it'd be fun. Still, she seemed baffled.
I fumbled, *Ms. Blume, we, the gays,*
love you. She wrote the message,
handed me my book and said,
I love most of you, too.

Garth Greenwell

True Image

Sweating in the sun on Boston Common, sick
with heat and melancholy, with the unobtainable
loveliness of unobtainable boys, sick with you
gilded in sun and sex beside me, I talk

as I always talk, from our trivium of beauty
and books and God advancing my veiled
stunted declarations, the ridiculous
dumbshow soliloquy of terrified love,

and turn, as however resisted or delayed always
I turn to your face, read and re-read past all
thought of discernment, greeted in terrible
leaping gladness wrenched and enraged—

to see, in the light reflected there, my image
on the curved surface of your sunglasses stretched
and distorted, mocking all my revisionist dreams
of self, for all the compulsive daily grind of discipline

and gym still out-sized and eager, swelled
with just-unslaughtered hope, like the *buffo* foil
for the heroic lover, whom you watch for now,
turning away to gaze out over the green.

After the Reading

On my friend's high balcony where we sat,
talking through cigarettes and drinks, he rose,
half turned away, and lit by a streetlamp's
solitary burn below, in casual nonsequitur
stripped off his shirt. He stood for a moment,
enjoying our surprise, the air's sudden erotic
snap, then lifted his glass half-ironically high—
as if toasting us, the night, as if toasting more
the careless thick American physique
he dared me not to adore.

                All that summer
he held himself before me like a lure.
I told him to sit down. I was tired, by then,
of flirtations empty and unactable as air,
his riskless game of hearts; and I was tired
of the pulse that leapt at his chest laid bare,
my eager plays for a bait I knew
would always be snatched back. And yet,
at the sight of him sprawled in the balcony chair,
how the prone heart leapt and leapt.

                    Later,
as he drove me home, too drunk to stand,
I watched the trees that lined the little streets
bend in the summer heat, their forms the same
though flush collegiate affluence passed
to misery, and then back. We didn't talk.
He was angry, or I was; but as he parked,
he mumbled something about my poems, some
praise I'd waited for all night, and then,
hand firm at my neck,

                he pulled me to his mouth.
His tongue was cold and stung of alcohol.
I slipped my hand beneath his shirt, feeling,
between the broad pectoral plates rising
with his breath, a sheen of sweat I wet
my fingers in, and beneath, past
the bunched abdominals covered lightly
with hair, past the bend of his waist,
irrepealable as any disillusionment,
the slack humiliating softness at his groin.

Steve Fellner

Ode to Agoraphobia

after Catullus

I am happy you kept my lover trapped
in his house, stuck
in front of the television, reluctant
to open the door for anyone
except the cable repairman. That was the best
gift for me when I deserted him,
thinking I needed to leave
our own tiny space, choosing lovers
who slept outdoors, all of us afraid
we were going to miss out
on something. Now I am
back. Don't let anyone
accuse you of being selfish. There isn't much
on this planet you can't see
on the back of a postcard. Even so, I am full
of so much doubt that when I wake up
I always run onto our porch to make sure
the universe is still there. I go
for long walks alone. The birds mimic
the way I drag my heels. I am relieved
that my beloved never wants me
to leave. From the window, he watches me
march away. He presses his forehead
against the glass. For a moment, my body resides
inside the circle of his eye.

"I'm working on a script now for Jerry Bruckheimer"

-CNN President Jon Klein in an interview for *Gotham* magazine

His opening
scene: evil
liberal politician
spontaneously
combusts
seconds after
giving a speech
about the dangers
of globalism
to an auditorium
full of sweet
octogenarians.
You can call
this an attention
getter, Jon learned
from a Saturday afternoon
screenwriting class
he attended instead of
preparing for the weekend
update: *Countdown
to the cease-fire
in Hezaballoh.* Seconds
tick off
as they do when the hero
dismantles the bomb
in those second-
rate movies
he's now smart enough
not to imitate.

Christian Gregory

Book Marks

> *a table at Buffalo's all night Greek Diner, the Towne Restaurant,*
> *after a sold out reading at the Albright-Knox Art Gallery in 1988*

who spiked his hair up like a petrified forest so when one would
          touch it they would feel the sting of nettles, who wore
          his sideburns long and suspenders tall, the thickness
          of yardsticks, who looked like an orthodox Amish
          hipster in black wool, who wore white gauze around
          his wrists, masking imaginary stigmata, who read Billy
          Budd, knowing all goodness will be destroyed, and
          beauty too. And it was my friend with me at the diner

who recalled his high school grappling matches and how he made
          everyone laugh on the bus because he was caustic not
          athletic, who now chain-smoked, and picked over
          Moby Dick and the elusive nature of symbols, and how
          Melville set it up that way to destroy the metaphor,
          like Ahab destroys the whale, and it was I

who replied, *Call me Crazy, but does Ahab destroy the whale, or does the*
          whale destroy him? Or is he just attached to it and carried off
          into oblivion? We finish our meal, our conversation,
          and as we made for the door, it is he,

who turned back Lot-like, and said, *It's him,* and it was, it was Allen
          Ginsberg, at the back table waiting for his quick
          dinner at a Greek diner. I said, *Let's go over* and he
          said, *No, we can't do that, that's rude*; and I said, *We're 20,*
          we're Whitman's Civil War soldiers. Follow me. And
          together, it was the both of us

who approached, and it was Ginsberg who lifted his eyes, each one
          of them in different directions. Lazy eye, Picasso eye,
          and it was he who saw many things at once, and he
          who motioned for us to sit down, and we did. And
          we talked, and he talked, as he picked over his plate of
          Mediterranean chicken and sipped his root beer

through a straw. (When they gave him the straw, it was cuffed with a white wrapper, and he left the wrapper by the outside of his spoon, and went to the root beer like a school boy.) And he asked us what we love and

what we loved was this: My friend loved Melville, and began to recite excerpts from his epic exegetic work on the breakdown of meaning. I think he said meta many times. I know he said meta. And what did I love? Shakespeare and his play of words, whose work I understood, and Hart Crane, whom I didn't understand, but whose beauty captured in that Walker Evans photo made me imagine he was mine. It was Crane, who journeyed to the edge of the dock drunk, calling for sailors, who wrote letters to his mother that read like words between newlyweds, and who in the thick of night on his honeymoon cruise cast himself over the railing into the waters below. And it was Ginsberg

who recited the opening stanzas of *The Bridge*, and we sat listening to his breath, and pace, and voice. And it was I

who said *What is your experience of drugs?* And he said, *Never recreationally. Only experientially. And always with Nature. Walk into a garden to witness the blades of grass and the weave of the spider. And the drug will take you from the spider to the thread, and from the thread to its gleam, and there, you'll stay in light.* And it was we three

who left to restaurant. And it was my friend and I who walked Alan to his hotel on Allen Street, and where years earlier Buffalo street walkers would idle looking for Johns. And it was we two

who talked after we dropped Alan off. And my friend said *He liked us.* And I said, *Of course he did. What's not to like?* And he said, *Would you do him?* And I thought, *What do I offer? What do I receive?* And he said, *Would you do him?*

And I said, *I don't think so.* And he said, *I would. I would totally do him.*
And it was I

who drove down Allen street the very next day, and I who saw my
friend walking away from Ginsberg's hotel, his hands
dug deep into his cords, a cigarette dangling like some
neo-beat. And it was I

who remembered that it was the two of them who made it to the
diner door together that night, and I who lagged
behind, lingering on Ginsberg's paper cuff that once
cradled his straw. It was I who witnessed the sheath
left behind, the one that readied the straw for his
open mouth, the same mouth that prayed and bayed.
And it was I who took that angled wrapper; it was I
who took it and put it between the pages of a book.

Charles Jensen

It Was October

I was love when I entered the bar
shivering in my thin t-shirt and ripped jeans
and I was love when I left that place, tugged along at the wrist
as though tied, with a man I did not know.

I was love there in the morning
when our sour kisses bore the peat of rotten leaves,
fallen October leaves. And it was love that we kissed anyway, not
       knowing
each other's names.

I was love in that bed
and I was love in the hall and down the stairs and into the freezing
       rain.

I was love with hands punched deep
into the pockets of a coat.
I was love coated in frozen rain.

Back home, I was love stripped of the cigarette-stung shirt, love
       pulling the stiff jeans from my legs.
I dried my hair and I was love.

It was October. What did I know of love that year,
shuddering in my nervous skin. Miles away, the boy was lashed to a
       fence and shivering.

Where that place turned red and the ground soaked through
with what he was, I was love.

What did I know of love then
but that it wasn't enough.

Selections from *"Safe"*

*

He goes into the truck
and all over town, faces pulled from the fray

iris out into pinprick holes in dark drapes, into windows and door
          frames
The sky blacks out

until it bears out its sad shroud
Small pairs of stars appear from horizon to horizon, blinking

The boys roll straight into black
three bullets shy

*

A gun has ownership over the hand, caresses the palm in such a way, speaks a message:

You are a killer
You enter the night as a man and come out red. You come out unshaken—

You come out of the night and someone else won't follow you—someone else
      has been bloodied
for twenty dollars and a pair of shoes

You are a killer
You came back red

*

As the night inked in above the mountains in a slow hand, could he
            recognize time:
could he then see light as it bleached the sky, burned out the stars

or was it
endless

expansive
hollowed out

did it swallow him
or did it chew

*

The skin's an ignoble thing until touched or torn—
even the most brutal contact has a shared warmth we can't ignore.

The men wear the purple hoods of night, their eyes wide and white.
The distances between us breathe too close—we share
            uncomfortable air, the body's steam

electrified by currents of pain
lit up in the skin

which claws at itself
tearing away from the bone

*

I believed we were safe before he died

Now I hear the cracking of pistols
in the break of a kiss

The soft, steady moan of the wind
in our lungs as we, entangled, pant

Now the event is inside us,
rank and sour. We carry its sadness like a gene.

Mónica Teresa Ortiz

Hanging Commando

means ride shotgun
hunt mermaids by pool tables in the King's X
enjoy a clandestine smoke in the lava pink
bathroom kiss heads of whores
lo-fi style with a romanticism
nobody can comprehend
don't pay money to Trannies
yanking hair on sidewalks outside
the New Old Plantation
leave behind a legacy of strippers
to steal your cell phone your money
and your virginity build a following
that eliminates ego with one swift critique
of sexual capability
Catholicism should prevent fucking
but that doesn't mean I can't keep hanging around
in hope that I can go
commando and stand a chance
with her

Kandinsky In New York

I like girls with guns.

Give me a vest engineered by Kevlar
so I can fall in love.

Talla

Soy el mar Pacífico Noreste
hacienda flotar los barcos sin tragármelos
cada milla que nos separa tiene
102,000 cuerpos de ballenas
moviendose azules en el agua

Entiende que el corazón de una ballena
azul es como un Volkswagen y más
liviano que el mío

Tamiko Beyer

If Oranges Opened

How do we measure the foam that slips from the beer?

By the tears that gather in the corners of old men eyes
and the sweat beading between the breasts
of women in sugar cane fields. By the bitter
sweep of air across tongue when the foam goes down.

How do oranges divide up sunlight in the orange tree?

Branch by branch, stem by stem,
skin by pocked skin, pulp by juicy pulp,
seed by seed by seed.

In the end, won't death be an endless kitchen?

The pots shining, the stove's blue flame burning clear,
cold, bright water from the tap, and oranges
round as morning piled in a bowl glazed green.

What is the distance in round meters between the sun and the oranges?

One round meter is the orange rolling
across your scarred back. Two round
meters is the orange splitting on your tender
tongue. Three round meters is the juice
I lick off your fingers, long as the sun's reach.

::   ::

When my first memory turned, it turned
and turned again into fragment. We are imprints
of bodies – bones on blankets on sand.

This heat wave lingers. The beer, more delicate
than promises. We navigate the world as it comes to us,
like dogs, following scent into shadowed paths.

If oranges opened their eyes, what would they see?

Note: Italicized lines from Pablo Neruda's *Book of Questions*.

How My Blue Behaves

Abysmally, all day, in the near-sly way
of a kid slipping out past curfew.
Hear the beer bottle clink? And the tip
of her cowboy boots against the bar?
My Blue behaves like a boy, a bad
one, a lying one, mouth as sweet as pie.
My Blue writes my heart off. As if we
didn't live sharing frying pans and falling
asleep holding hands. Somebody's devil
talked to somebody's god and now my Blue
behaves like a wild dog galloping across a meadow.
Take my beer bottle, take my day, it's just about done.
Sing it: Flip cap, cap tip, tipper, tip her.
We've got to get out of here – my Blue's
got tears running down her nose
and there's not a handkerchief
stashed in anyone's pocket.

The Swaying Was

sun through makeshift curtains our mouths raw sheets damp days pass
the phone rings her skin tinder my own salt we drench what feels like
begging what feels like fruit's pulp I go down on her burst against my
tongue

city stinks high summer the pretty boys drink chilled chardonnay at
sidewalk cafes she and I sweat all extravagances into each other's wild
pores

:: ::

                    under lemon trees
                    tranced by bold press
                    women's bodies
                    it should
                    have always been
                    me knowing
                    there were patios
                    like this women like this
                    left trembling
                    I drink night clear
                    neck curve like colt
                    and blush

:: ::

        we curled commas my right hand cupping her left breast nipple
softening against my palm we drift

:: ::

when matched femme to
clean sway   the swagger
this fierce yes
bare shoulders and thin
heels yes   calves' sluicing line
I'm her curl as salt fit
and come press
evening strands

:: ::

i.	if there were a thread and a button hook they would appear now
ii.	the subject being introduced and wandered away from leading to other things and returning transformed to wander away again
iii.	the strange way you do when you want her so much you take her skin between your teeth and bite hard
iv.	just about any space two bodies can occupy
v.	the Japanese say "I'm going"
vi.	vibrators
vii.	dear buzz, my identity's been slid out
viii.	if gender were fixed it would now be introduced and then transformed
ix.	straddle grasp her cock and watch the terrible beauty of her face twist
x.	star fruit split open

Julie Weber

Digitalis

I think to myself, I am not brave enough
(naïve enough) to keep taking this digitalis,
both medicine and poison.

I am sitting on the floor in the hall
after her call, trying to find
the wall to steady me, to stop
my heart from falling through the crawlspace.
I don't know where the ground is,
can't find a catch to hold onto.

In my mind, the phone keeps ringing
in rapid succession, the way she calls
eight times a night, keeping me tied
into her nest of complexes and complexities,
need and passion, knotted around the vine
of "too many differences" and "we should just be friends".

The immediacy of the little purple bells
are ringing everywhere, and I can't answer them tonight.

Will I or won't I find, after the shock,
the beauty of tall spikes swaying again
in my garden, broad leaves, like green sandals
that climb up or down soldier-like stalks,
little cups, farther up,

                              that both steady
the heart or send it into blurred vision,
the opening or closing of, between us,
this circulatory valve.

Francisco Aragón

Midtown Tryptich

      Broadway
past Lincoln
      Center and the wind

is up so seems
      to speak
saw you

      through the glass
standing in line
      I swear a quiver

rose
      to your lips
you were

      leafing through his book…
—years
      it's been years

since Corona
      Heights, backing
into him: dribble,

      hook, swish…
…that beige
      comfy couch,

sipping a stem
      of wine, his cat
in my lap

*

The Townhouse
Saturday night—shoulder

to shoulder pushing
towards the piano he

stops to squeeze
by; his eyes mine

clench unclench…
…What was it we found

in common over
drink smoke talk?

A college campus
—his son, his daughter

*

Earlier that night I rose
to the city's surface
steam through the grate, crossed
crossed again down 7th

past Carnegie Hall, the greek
joint as imagined, chic
—unlike the shirt
D wore (the fur

of his arms) at Castro
and Market waiting
for the light: words were struck
like steel and flint

that distant August day…Then
his visit to Spain, mine
to New Canaan—walking
through the Morgan

with him. And what

our mouths unfurled
across a table of olives
years later—last night…

Dropping me off at 58th he
reaches for the door
I'm fumbling to open, leans
close and plants

what I've missed

all these years

Jee Leong Koh

Leave with Nothing

Who needs ten shirts when two will do, one on the back,
the other in the wash? Who needs five pairs of jeans?
Who, in his right mind, needs two pairs of underwear?
Too many! Who goes to the laundromat in briefs?

I have lived with little, I will live with less.
These books, accumulated like a secret vice,
seduced even the saint, and so must be reduced
to ten, no, five, no, two, no, no, how about one?

None. So, when a man needs you, he says, to go,
same man who needed you a year ago to stay,
you won't leave with a rucksack and three shopping bags,
but fill your empty pockets with your empty hands.

You have lived with little, you will live with less.
Welcome, welcome, welcome to your new address.

Christian Gullette

Postcard Never Mailed

The volcano cap hoards its ice.
Clouds find a pregnant pause.

The sun reaches cruising altitude.
Gnats prepare for its descent.

If it rained like they say
I wouldn't be able to lie here

by this lake pretending I can
remain still my whole life.

Am I really the person
who just followed a stranger

into a rusty stall above a drain?
I must have thought he was wood

because I leaned against him
while he fumbled with a wet

stubborn knot. I looked up
as if down didn't exist

but he was already moving,
a boy diving for a coin.

The richest man in America
lives across the lake in a house

that has been programmed to think.
But I am unable to think.

That house can turn on twenty thousand lights
that will blink when desire moves.

Movie Set

Overnight they repainted the theater,
but you say it like it was a bad thing,
waking up to Castro Street's facelift,
transported thirty years back

to youthful poses in an old yearbook,
forgotten store fronts and VW bugs
superimposed over porn and Starbucks.
You haven't time for nuisance,

the parlor tricks of resurrection.
And Milk's old camera shop?
If you're going do it, at least get it right!
It's the past without any of its demands.

When any world is called for,
we paint ourselves into it,
the museum of a carefree time
curiously cleaner than it ever was,

an amusement park's Tudor Village,
loudspeakers concealed in its tower
belting out frivolous music
while families picnic on the green.

Only the bank's row of ATMs,
excluded from some exterior shot,
provides the beginning of any truth,
but you'd already decided what to keep.

Patient Zero

How did you become the beginning?

Even after death, everything you divide is null.
Did you teach our bodies to declare war,
to desire the wound?

The tale's inaccuracy doesn't matter,
it's the betrayal.
You liked surprising tricks with the lesions.
When asked if sex was your revenge,
you said no, unrepentant. *Heaven doesn't understand it.*

Do you still see your body in the world?
A flight attendant again, surveying your handiwork?

We don't want to remember you.
We've scratched out your likeness
and left an empty set, an empty cartouche.
We pretend your story is not our story.

Eduardo C. Corral

To the Beastangel

> *...unconscionable musics*
> —Ronald Johnson

A pouring of milk among the reeds, the neck of a swan. I float
   on a pond. Nude. Obese. Around

my throat, on a leather cord, an amulet carved from soap.
   Myth-haired, eyes shut,

you stand on the bank. In your hands a finch. I call your name.
   You release the finch. It wings toward me,

settles on my chest. It pecks and pecks at the moles on my skin,
   swallows the moles

like seeds. I asked once for a father. You gave me a wreath.
   I asked once for a sonnet. You

peeled back the skin and muscle of your left hand: fourteen bones.
   One by one the moles

on my body disappear. Leaving me immaculate. Leaving me
   ravenous. I call your name. The finch

flies back to you. You crush it. Bright blood, blue guts. I asked
   once for grace. You dusted

my face with ash. I ask, I ask, I ask...You step into the pond.
   Hair dissipating like smoke.

Eyes still shut. The reeds tick and tick. At your touch, my nipples
   open like bird beaks.

Mary Meriam

Sea de Sade

unmoored from the mother ship of culture
            - Camille Paglia

wallow in Sadean sadomasochistic chthonian nature
                    - Mary Rose Kasraie, in *Sexual Personae*

Marquise, dear darling bitch of decadence,
enough about your love for ancient Rome.
Let's reminisce about our close events.
You chased me, caught me, slayed me, brought me home,
proud master hunter in pursuit of prey.
Fainting I followed, wide-eyed, silent, high
on scotch and cigarettes. Quick came the day
you dumped me with a strangely sweet goodbye.
"Come here and sit," you said, "upon my lap."
"Oh, I'm too big," I moaned, "so tall, so big.
I can't." Was I so big? Well, no. Tap-tap,
you tapped, and so I sat, a sinking brig,
unmoored from the mother ship of culture, drunk
on masochism, and by a sadist sunk.

Orphic Chant

Let singer seek the way to hell,
and bring her back, and bring her back.
Let singer sound the hole of black,
and make her well, and make her well.
Let singer charm the deadly dell,
for knick the singer has a knack.
Let singer seek the way to hell,
and bring her back, and bring her back.
Let singer strike the silver bell.
Let singer ride the railroad track.
Let singer face the devil pack.
Let singer seek the way to hell,
and bring her back, and bring her back.

Matthew Hittinger

Bufeo Colorado

Unlike the werewolf, the Amazon's ruddy dolphin-
man becomes human when the moon grows full;
once ashore, he dons a Panama hat to cover his
                    bald pate's blow hole.

            Pacaya river names *Alfaro*
                        broken into *Amazon* broken
into pencil lead tributaries

                    the *Orinoco* mission to find
                                boto a total mess Mateus
            guessed *tonight I will write off my quest*

            confessed *I am a failed animal*
                    scientist
                                his blue-black curls lunar-
frosted as he wandered shirt open

            off the town's esplanade, back licked
                        by shadows chanting
                                Anthony de
                        Santos, John, e Peter.

            Mateus watched light
shards slice tannin-stained waters. He knelt,
            a pink wisp split the surface.

            My face? Swallowed he thought.

                    His fingertips edged
light inch deep ten fractured stubs pumping.

A voice from the river caught
     on the ribbed fronds above him.

    Yemaya he prayed *Yemaya* he
       raved tearing a page
          from his notebook
       casting it on the waves.

        He turned away, caught
           a glimpse of white

    straw, a brim splintered through vines,
  followed the Panama to bonfires.

      An accordion tightened its whine.

   Hips *dançar!* ground hips. Mateus's
     blue sought out dark
        eyes under white brim

    but when asked *Who are you?* Bufeo
      simply bobbed his brim.
Only recently come ashore, he did not know

the language of men, his pupils reflecting moon
    and fire like wind
       off a hurricane-churned sea.

    While Mateus made love to Bufeo that night
      the brim stayed.

Bufeo woke sweat-soaked noticed pale
   light at the window felt his hat
      slowly lift.

     Eyes darted
       to the clock.

A finger rimmed the exposed blow-hole.

Bufeo did not run could
say nothing but wait for sleep to take,
to slip out from his arms
slink down to the river, Mateus

left to dream of pink ripple
black cleft.

Amazon glimmered red. Bufeo
swam, blood close under skin, Mateus

panting in time to see *boto* hump
break breath hole closed open

closed again.

Two Black Swans

Black swan loves black swan if love
is the word for what swans feel. Can one
know for sure what one swan feels
let alone two? They face each other
raise wings expose ivory
underthings flap distal primaries
secondaries white inner

coverts tertial edges curled.
What is primary in this gesture.
Manus like a hand and wrist
set to greet. What is secondary.
Bend of second joint both seen
only in flight. And tertiary.
Curled edges ape repeated

calls that high-pitched melodic
trumpeting from the extended neck
the lifted-up vermilion
bill that says love and love again love
too. Each swan utters garbled
wordless sounds inflected to say more
than a word stretched to a point

where it has lost shade colored
degrees like the gray fringe on sooty
bodies. Calls do not carry
far but far enough to hear a tint
of desire the white sub-
terminal band brightening in red
irises beyond the red

tip reflection of sameness

be it desire or image each
        swan doubled in the water
in the eye. And what is primary.
        Both are male longer necks bent
                over a trail of cygnets who do
                        not seem to care or differ

        from other cygnets. Alpha
fathers mean larger lands better food
        higher survival rates but
do swans respect envy status does
        the surrogate mother hate
                or love swan fathers her adopted
                        cygnets. Are the chased away

        couple bothered is their love
better or equal secondary
        when two males abduct laid eggs
incubate hatch feed and raise the clutch
        together duties shared more
                equally. Perhaps that fact is that :
                        tertiary like the Uw

        Oykangand Uw Olkola
who named black swan *inh owonhdhom* as
        magical as the Latin
Cygnus atratus. And yet what text
        books ban censor or forget
                cannot lessen innate attraction
                        to the subtle wonder in

        paradox the idea
unbound like the reflected S-curve
        of bodies : wave-like they dip
heads necks draw near the broken image
        of one glued back together
                bills bugling *love black swan*
                        in the other's rippled countenance.

Linda Benninghoff

Going for Chemo

There was
the silence
of the pots
after they were washed,
put on the rack to dry.

That evening a dead seagull lay
flat like paper on the causeway.

You touched the gray
in your splintery, falling-out hair.
We were going out
getting ice cream.
Back inside
the teapot
made a sound
I remembered
long after that day,
a sound like robins praying.

Reply to Rilke

Not to hear even one's first name mentioned.
This must be death. In the underworld,
I cannot glimpse the spring coming,
smell the fresh-cut grass.
Dandelions don't spot the field.
Who are the angels? Do they come to us
even in death, and slowly lift us
from oblivion?

These flowers shine brightly. They take the stars
away.

I fear the winter but the spring more.
The first crocus bloom is
terrible under the March sun.
I feel the dim shoots' change,
pushing from underneath, the soil
growing moist instead of caked and hard.

the thread

the thread

always goes back to janina siedlewski.
grandma.
and the net i attempt to catch her stories in.

here's one, translated by
her daughter/my mother/aleksandra.
translated, not from polish to english
but rather
from untold/silence
to
a theory
a suspicion
a stabinthedark:

she got down
with a priest.
there's no reference
to whether it was coercive
or an act of desire
or a mix of both.
and her child
because of wedlock
was taken.
always mysteriously taken.

i imagine hitler
swooping down on baby bogusz
like a bird of prey
maniacal cackles tumbling
from his orangeyellow beak

taken.
i imagine the pope

clicking his tongue
pointing his finger
at teenage janina
before grabbing
the boy
and tucking him into
holy starched folds
of his white cassock.

taken.
i imagine the stork
flying in
claiming, "sorry, we made a mistake"
or perhaps, "sorry, you made a mistake"
or rather, "sorry, the roman catholic church
made a mistake but we're going to blame it on you."

here's another translation
from word to image:
yellowing black and white
poland.
1940's.
she's on a cruiser bike
button-down cotton dress, worn out laced-up boots and
white rose-appliquéd scarf over her head
tidy knot at the neck.
the road a dry dirt gravel.
enter soldiers.
hitler's soldiers.
they scare her enough
that the frost of fear
settles
somewhere so deep in her bones
preserving the ache
that she's still telling the story
60 years later
to a certain grandkid.
the one with the holey net.

this one is not so much story
as it is recipe, tradition:

kapusta.
[potatoes mashed with peas and sauerkraut.]
mushroom barley soup.
steamed cabbage rolls.
poppy seed cake.
four generations
spooning this history
into their mouths
around the same table
24th of december.
every year.

things found:

1970's porn:
1 new year's issue playboy
1 full color book, down-at-the-ranch-themed

drafts of a suicide note
deep in chris's closet
stored with an array of
bottles
cleaning products

ami's diary and its' key
which included illustrations of codewords:
breadsticks (cigarettes)
compacts (emptied of powder:
drug-carrying-device)
hairspray (alcohol)
razor blades

mom's menstrual calendar

mom's journal:
hard-pressed handwriting
silenced truths spilled

dad's veitnam photo album
images held to paper by tongue-licked
photo-corners
semi-scandalous pictures
of nightclub dancers
feathers, glitter, pinkorange lights
heels and legs

things never found:

dad's gun
(which, from hazy memory,
i have reason to believe exists)

sex toys and any form of birth control
(which, i have reason to believe,
doesn't exist)

Jen Currin

Chronicle: The Sexual

Thirst is occasionally intelligent.

One of those scars you meet on a beach.

She was a graffiti artist & recently jailed.

Some use the word "gifted."
I never know what it means.

In a box of free books:
fault ink and grammar trauma.

Excited is a state:
Your ballroom, your bike, your gown.

Thoughts lie on top of each other.
No—nothing so orderly as this,
and dangerous, a performance.

It starts with smashing perfume bottles on the floor.
Then blowing on microphones.

No one wants to talk about the erotica of the absurd—
but what sort of room spills wine like this?

You took classes on Shakespeare & dated volunteers.

She had been lying, & would continue to.

Chronicle: Blame

Cooking in a white dress.
A while dress.

It will be karma, my costume
& speech. Sister humming
son to sleep.

A gap, again,
between "self" and "world."

I am this mushroom, this potato
torn from the front garden.

Also listing on the couch,
I am the dumbest theorist.

Repetition again. Like
an erotic riddle: lake, lake, water.

Theory drips; strong coffee;
coffin brashly in the rain.

Huddled over, handed in.
Before communism,
we called it "sharing."

My neighbor leaves pictures of a rainbow
over our house & crayon drawings.

The individual can be a monstrous thing.
Like your husband's drug habit & death.

After he left, nights
of apologies: *Can I sleep next to you?*

And you: *Yes, but carefully.*
I am very afraid.

Dreamt him scrubbed, nervous,
new suit, suitcases.

—*Where are you going?*
—*I don't know, but it's ok.*

Every night we meditate with bones.

Mop the contagious hospital in a while dress.

Who will address this?

Like fault, you find me.

A fly worries the front door

I was for a night.

And then I woke up.

On every campus—
prideful, joyful.

I am the bride of bullshit.
Which is why this letter:

Just yesterday on my bicycle
I remembered why this body.

A drink of water.
Nothing to say.

In a closed way, I understand you.

Any of my class might be watering
their plants right now.

We disappoint each other at every page.

Never Suggest We Are the Missionary Position

Joke: Soul veers into bar,
lights drink on fire,
starts fight with body.

Contrary shapes, eyes of snow-owls.

What makes the body?
Surely not
the periphery dresses.

I'm all caught up in your hair.

The phone booth. Both of us.
The way you put it: *confused*.
Confined? By shadows.

I felt elephant for awhile, then forgot.

No noodles too thin for supper.
The body bathing
in consciousness. Next.

Nest on windowsill. My mother's
pathology: *Take a little piece
of the unforgiving parts*.

Each thing ending, turning to water.

I blink, a fruit you call *detail*,
as birds to water.
It suggests the globe, your love.

D.M. Solis

My Knee

I think a flea
has bit my knee
from my dog
in the carpet.

I never see
any on her
but this one roams free
to graze on me
whenever it feels like it.

I get my bread
from the day-old bakery.
The bread there
is good as any
that sits in my fridge
for days since you left
before I remember
to eat.

And see how I
just caught that flea
and cracked it
between my thumbs.
See how I grieve
when I think about
time

before you left—
down on the carpet
caressing my knee

pointing to your bed
and telling me
when you returned
when you returned
when you returned…

Dean Kostos

At the Barber's

I wait for Zoya—Russian for Zoë—I wait for life.
Every time I arrive, her hair's a different shade of marigold:
trumpet, egg yolk, cognac. She's been my barber
for years. Her chair's at the end

of the room, near hooks where jackets and sweaters
hang. Seated in her swiveling throne, I watch other patrons
in the mirror without turning my head, simply gazing
at reflections, and reflections of reflections.

I observe the dark–haired, young barber,
his chair next to Zoya's. Although he's also Russian, he speaks
English without an accent. His tea-colored
eyes are large, his lips a cursive lowercase "m."

His nostrils seem to have been shaped by pressing
an index finger into wet clay. Covered
with silky, black hair, his arms are "in velvet"—said of stags'
antlers when spring scents the air with musk.

It's been a long winter, and I'm here to be sheared
in anticipation of spring. As Zoya artfully clips and trims, I look
in the mirror and notice a man in his mid-thirties easing
into the adjacent chair. He's noticed me

noticing him, yet won't return
my stare, as if not to admit *I know who we are.*
Will he get his goatee trimmed? Is it dyed? Several shades
darker than the hair on his head. His features are rounded,

solid. He engages the barber in male banter—
artificial, learned, scripted—to fit in, to entice.
And it works. The two shift from politics
to weather, the customer closing

his eyes as the barber glides the electric razor
over the back of his head. His hair seems to crumble, falling
away like steel shavings to a magnet. While Zoya
meticulously snips short hair around my ears, I glance

into the mirror to watch the man who won't acknowledge me.
He's murmuring something as the barber lathers
the back of his neck. With tongs, the barber fishes into a jar
of blue disinfectant, retrieving a straight razor,

erasing foam and hair from his newly revealed
flesh. The customer's eyes are closed.
(I can't look away!)
The barber massages the smooth skin of the man's neck

with lilac-scented astringent. I imagine the barber bending
down, planting a kiss, then pivoting
the chair, and pressing his lips to the man's mouth.
But realizing the cut-and-shave ritual

has ended, the client opens his eyes
and resumes the formality of feigned conversation.
Cape removed, he regards himself in the mirror,
thanks the barber, and dissolves

into brisk March air. Having tamed my hair, Zoya
wields a hand-mirror like a priestess, exposing
the back of my neck—
place I can't see for myself.

Blas Falconer

If

Years later, you still wonder. Had only you kissed
that morning, everything would

be different now: train routes,
the way rain falls into the field for months,

your calloused heels. When did you grow
so tall? Maybe the walk would have been

shorter longer, the letters home
less/more frequent—hours in the phone booth

calling out as others paced the dark,
pulling their coats closed, bowing their heads

to the wind. Where is he now, the other young man
written in no book? Where you left him,

asleep, half dressed. Smoke stacks stretch
into the sky of every city.

This is the cause of all your pain
and joy, neither of which lasts very long.

To press the air, to bless the silhouette,

the owl and the field mice: that argument—
and spare no speck of dust or fleck of light,

all fair and foul, lush and bare: the vine
that takes the barn, the nest inside the brush

(the dog's muzzle soaked in blood);
to resist caving in, taking comfort

in routine, socks sorted, shrinking from
disorder; to cut the fruit and not think

of the heart, to think of it and not flinch
or flinch and cut through its core all the same,

you wake up, walk out late at night, still dazed
and stand in the yard, which, at day, lolls

under heat, the red trumpet blossoms bob,
where, at dusk, strays rise from the tall grass

to wander the streets, a fearless pack
in search of food among the trash we've left

exposed. Below, the city sleeps. You'll test
yourself the way you always have, a boy

stepping into the dark and the story
whatever it was. Whatever it was.

Still Life with Orange

—for Joseph, who wants a child of his own

The fruit on the plate is split in two.

An open hand holds the air

or the shadow of the head that hangs above.

The window gives a square of light.

Someone may be crying there:

a white blossom.

              The blossom end

looks like the human navel

because a second fruit fails

to grow within the first.

The seedless fruit cannot bear fruit.

It sings in the mouth of one

Contributors

Brian Leary is the Managing Editor of *42opus* (www.42opus.com). He lives in Brooklyn.

Elizabeth J. Colen currently a freelance writer/editor, has been the recipient of several awards and special notices, most recently shortlisted for Akron University Press's Akron Poetry Prize. Her work recently appears in *Exquisite Corpse, Redivider, RATTLE, The Portland Review, Fifth Wednesday Journal, Pebble Lake Review, Juked, Knockout, Spoon River Poetry Review, So To Speak*, and others.

RJ Gibson appears online at *Six Sentences* and *qarrtsilluni* and is forthcoming in *Knockout* and *BLOOM* and the anthology *Diva: 65 Gay Men on the Women Who Inspire Them* (U. of Wisconsin Press.) In August, 2008 he was a Lambda Literary Retreat Fellow in poetry and in January 2009 began his first residency in Warren Wilson's MFA Program for Writers.

Carol Guess' fifth book of poetry, *Tinderbox Lawn* (Rose Metal Press) was published in November 2008. She is also the author of two novels, a memoir, and the poetry collection *Femme's Dictionary* (Calyx Books). She teaches Queer Studies and Creative Writing at Western Washington University, and lives in Bellingham with her spouse, writer Elizabeth Colen.

Jeremy Halinen is coeditor and cofounder of *Knockout Literary Magazine* (knockoutlit.org). Some of his recent poems appear in *Arroyo Literary Review; Best Gay Poetry 2008; Dos Passos Review; Pontoon: an anthology of Washington State Poets, Number Ten; Quarter After Eight;* and *Rio Grande Review.*

Christine Leclerc is currently pursuing an MFA in Creative Writing at the University of British Columbia. Her work has appeared in *Dig, FRONT, FU, Interim, Memewar, Pistola, subTerrain, terry*, and the Worksound gallery. She is the author of *Counterfeit*, a book of poetry published by Capilano University Editions in 2008.

Julie R. Enszer took her MFA from the University of Maryland and is enrolled currently in the PhD in Women's Studies at the University of Maryland. Her poetry has previously been published in *Iris: A Journal About Women, Room of One's Own, Long Shot,* the *Web Del Sol Review,* and the *Jewish Women's Literary Annual.* She has poems forthcoming in the *Women's Review of Books* and *Feminist Studies.* She is a regular book reviewer for the *Lambda Book Report* and *Calyx.* You can read more of her work at www.JulieREnszer.com.

Scott Hightower's third collection, *Part of the Bargain,* received Copper Canyon's 2004 Hayden Carruth Award and his translations from Spanish have garnered a Willis Barnstone translation prize. His poems have appeared in the *Yale Review, Salmagundi, The Paris Review, Gulf Coast, The Southwest Review, Ploughshares, AGNI,* and other journals throughout the country. His reviews have appeared in *Library Journal, Coldfront Magazine, Boxcar Poetry Review, Chelsea,* and the *Manhattan Review.*

Brent Goodman is the author of *The Brother Swimming Beneath Me* (Black Lawrence Press, 2009) and two chapbooks: *Wrong Horoscope* (Thorngate Road, 1999), winner of the Frank O'Hara Award, and *Trees are the Slowest Rivers* (Sarasota Poetry Theatre, 1998). He lives and works in Rhinelander, Wisconsin.

C. Dale Young currently practices medicine, edits poetry for *New England Review,* and teaches in the Warren Wilson College MFA Program for Writers. His books of poetry include *The Day Underneath the Day* (Northwestern 2001) *The Second Person* (Four Way Books 2007) and *TORN,* to be published by Four Way Books in early 2012.

Dustin Brookshire is the founder and editor of *Limp Wrist* as well as a poet and activist. His work has appeared in numerous online journals, including *SubtleTea, ToasterMag,* and *Atlanta Rainbow Muse.* His blog, *I Was Born Doing Reference in Sin,* has made it to the floor of the Georgia Senate, and he is happy to keep elected officials on their toes.

Garth Greenwell has new and recent poems in *Salmagundi, New Orleans Review, Poetry International, TriQuarterly, and Boston Review.* He holds an MFA from Washington University in St. Louis and an MA from Harvard. His work has received the Grolier Prize, the Rella Lossy Award, and three Pushcart nominations; this summer he was the John Atherton Scholar in Poetry at Bread Loaf.

Steve Fellner's book of poems *Blind Date with Cavafy* was released by Marsh Hawk Press (2006).

Christian Gregory lives and teaches in New York City. Currently, he is pursuing his Master of Letters from the Bread Loaf School of English, concentrating on object-relations and identity in Late Victorian and Early 20th Century British Literature. He has moderated *The Glass House Reading Series* for two summers at Bread Loaf, was awarded a 2006 NEH grant for study, and was a semi-finalist for the Bechtel Prize. He is currently working on his first book of poems titled *Retroactivity*.

Charles Jensen is the author of *The First Risk* (Lethe Press), forthcoming in 2009, and three chapbooks, including *Living Things*, which won the 2006 Frank O'Hara Chapbook Award, and *The Strange Case of Maribel Dixon* (New Michigan Press). The recipient of an artist's project grant from the Arizona Commission on the Arts, he now lives in the Washington, DC area, where he directs The Writer's Center. His poetry has appeared in *Bloom, The Journal, New England Review, West Branch,* and *Willow Springs.*

Mónica Teresa Ortiz has been published in *La Palabra, Bordersenses, In the Grove,* and *Borderlands.* She is also the author of the chapbook *On a Greyhound Straight from the 915* (Finishing Line Press). She blogs at http://watchastheempirefalls.blogspot.com and currently lives in Austin, Texas.

Tamiko Beyer's work has appeared or is forthcoming in numerous journals and anthologies, including *Crab Orchard Review, Copper Nickel, The Drunken Boat, The Progressive, Gay and Lesbian Review,* and *Cheers to Muses: Contemporary Work by Asian American Women.* Her manuscript, *three stamens, seventeen syllables,* was a finalist in the 2007 New River Press Many Voices Project competition. She is currently a Chancellor's Fellow at Washington University in St. Louis where she is pursing an M.F.A.

Julie Weber is a Clinical Social Worker living in a small university town in the Southern Oregon mountains. Her previous work has appeared in *HLFQ*, *Sophie's Wind*, and appears at *butchculture.com*, as well as in local and regional newsmagazines and print journals.

Francisco Aragón is the author of, *Puerta del Sol* (Bilingual Press) and editor of the award-winning, *The Wind Shifts: New Latino Poetry* (University of Arizona Press). He directs *Letras Latinas*, the literary program of the Institute for Latino Studies at the University of Notre Dame and is the editor of CANTO COSAS, a book series from *Bilingual Press* featuring new Latino and Latina poets. He is a member of the Macondo Writing Workshop. For more information, visit: *http://franciscoaragon.net*

Jee Leong Koh is the author of *Payday Loans* (Poets Wear Prada Press, 2007). His new book of poems *Equal to the Earth* is forthcoming from the same press in March 2009. He lives in New York City, and blogs at *http://jeeleong.blogspot.com*.

Christian Gullette is currently studying poetry in the Warren Wilson College MFA Program for Writers. He lives in San Francisco.

Eduardo C. Corral was born and raised in Casa Grande, Arizona. He recently completed his first collection of poems.

Mary Meriam's chapbook, *The Countess of Flatbroke* (afterword by Lillian Faderman), was published in 2006 by Modern Metrics in New York City. Her poems and essays have been published in *Literary Imagination*, *The Gay & Lesbian Review*, *Windy City Times*, *A Prairie Home Companion*, *Light Quarterly*, *Street Spirit*, and *Umbrella*, among others.

Matthew Hittinger is the author of *Pear Slip* which won the Spire Press 2006 Chapbook Award. He has received a Hopwood Award from the University of Michigan, the Kay Deeter Award from the journal *Fine Madness*, and three Pushcart nominations. His work appears in many journals including *American Letters & Commentary*, *Center*, *DIAGRAM*, *Mantis*, *Meridian*, *Memorious*, *Michigan Quarterly Review*, *MiPOesias*, *Oranges & Sardines* and elsewhere, and is forthcoming in *Knockout*, *Dusie* and *Phoebe* as well as included in the anthology *Best New Poets 2005*. He lives and works in New York City.

Linda Benninghoff has published four chapbooks of poetry, *The Street Where I Was a Child, Departures, The Spaces Between Things* and *Elegies for Mary* which won a chapbook competition in Kritya, India. The winner of the Poetry Super Highway contest and shortlisted for the Cinnamon Poetry Book Prize, she is assistant poetry editor at womenwriters.net.

Franciszka Voeltz co-created the *Brontosaruaus Word Processing Exchange*, a queer literary/performance ensemble, and serves as a *Write Around Portland* workshop facilitator. Her poems have appeared in several publications including *Apothecary* (a fact-simile publication), *Voicecatcher, Sheepshead Review* and *Analecta Literary Journal*.

Jen Currin lives in Vancouver, B.C., where she teaches writing and tries to grow vegetables in her front yard. She has published two books of poems, *The Sleep of Four Cities* and *Hagiography*, and has one forthcoming, *The Inquisition Yours*.

D.M. Solis is a technical writer/editor by trade and the author of the column, "Intensely Latina" in *The Lesbian News Magazine.*, an international print magazine. She works at the California Institute of Technology (Caltech).

Dean Kostos is the author of three books of poetry, most recently *Last Supper of the Senses*. He co-edited *Mama's Boy: Gay Men Write About Their Mothers* and edited *Pomegranate Seeds: An Anthology of Greek American Poetry*. His work has appeared, or is forthcoming, in *Barrow Street, Boulevard, Chelsea, Cimarron Review, The Cincinnati Review, Confrontation, Euphony, Rattapallax, Southwest Review, Stand Magazine, Talisman, The Wallace Stevens Journal, Western Humanities Review*, and on Oprah Winfrey's Web site *Oxygen.com*.

Blas Falconer is the author of *A Question of Gravity and Light* (University of Arizona Press). He teaches at Austin Peay State University and is the poetry editor of *Zone 3: A Literary Journal*.

Miguel Murphy is the author of *A Book Called Rats*, a collection of poems from Eastern Washington University Press and Curating Editor for *Pistola: A Literary Review of Poetry Online* (www.pistolamag.org).

1924515